STATE BOARD FOR
TECHNICAL AND
COMPREHENSIVE EDUCATION

W9-CPH-237

Ancient Pottery

Other titles in this series:

Cassell's Introducing Archaeology Series

Ancient Pottery

RIVKA GONEN

Cassell · London

CASSELL & COMPANY LTD
35 Red Lion Square, London WC1R 4SG
Sydney, Auckland
Toronto, Johannesburg

Designed by Ofra Kamar

9085

© 1973 BY G.A. The Jerusalem Publishing House,
    39, Tchernechovski St., P.O. Box 7147, Jerusalem.

First published in Great Britain 1973

I.S.B.N. 0 304 29266 4

Printed by Japhet Press, Ltd., Givataim
PRINTED IN ISRAEL

F. 873

CONTENTS

INTRODUCTION

The production of pottery is one of the oldest crafts people have invented. Pottery vessels, made of clay and hardened by fire, fulfil basic needs of every human society — needs for storing, preparing and consuming food. The potter's craft, utilizing ubiquitous and therefore cheap raw materials, became soon after its invention one of the most common and widespread crafts and contributed an important share to the improvement of life in ancient times.

The importance of pottery to the study of the past springs first of all from the profusion of clay vessels wherever people once lived. Not only were pottery vessels very common in antiquity, but a fired pottery vessel is almost indestructible. A vessel can break, but its sherds do not disintegrate, corrode or rot even if they are buried in the earth for thousands of years. The study and interpretation of these large quantities of ancient pottery is complex and many-sided. The pottery vessel, carrying the mind and hand of the ancient potter, allows us to glimpse into the taste and requirements of ancient societies and thus gain a better understanding of their culture. The technical aspects of pottery making, the tools used by the potter to form and fire his products, add yet another important angle — the technological angle — to the study of life in ancient times. Last but not least come the enjoyment of the personal contact with common, everyday artefacts used thousands of years ago, and the aesthetic experience derived from the appreciation of the qualities of the form and decoration of the ancient vessel. The recognition of the invaluable contribution of pottery vessels to the study of the past opened new vistas in archaeological research, which strives to reconstruct all aspects of ancient life.

The following pages will deal with the techniques of pottery-making with several of the possible modes of interpreting pottery vessels and the changes occurring in their style from period to period.

The work of the potter, giving shape to formless, worthless material, has attracted the imagination of biblical prophets and authors who used the potter's craft as an allegory for the relationship between God and man. The very creation of man is described in terms of the potter:

> By the sweat of thy brow shalt thou eat bread till thou return into the ground; for out of it wast thou taken; for dust thou art and unto dust thou shalt return.
>
> Genesis 3:19

Job reacts to this metaphor by pleading with God:

> Thy hands have framed me and fashioned me together round about; yet Thou dost destroy me. Remember, I beseech Thee, that Thou hast fashioned me as clay: and wilt Thou bring me into dust again?
>
> Job 10:8–9

A realistic description of the potter's workshop is given by the prophet Jeremiah in these words:

> Then I went down to the potter's house, and behold, he was at his work on the wheels, and whensoever the vessel that he made of the clay was marred in the hand of the potter he made it again another vessel, as seemed good to the potter to make it.

But this description has an allegorical meaning, as shown by the following passage:

> Then the words of the Lord came unto me saying, O house of Israel, cannot I do with you as this potter? saith the Lord. Behold, as the clay in the potter's hand, so are ye in My hand, O house of Israel.
>
> Jeremiah 18:3–6

While this passage stresses the plastic qualities of clay, the prophets were also impressed by the worthlessness of the finished product, the fired vessel, or better still, the broken potsherds. According to this metaphor, Isaiah scolds the people of Israel and reminds them of their humble status in the eyes of God:

> Woe unto him that striveth with his Maker, as a potsherd with the potsherds of the earth! Shall the clay say to him that fashioneth it, What makest thou? or thy work, He hath no hands?
>
> Isaiah 45:9

The ancient Egyptians also attributed great importance to the potter's craft. They showed the ram-horned god Khnum forming mankind on the potter's wheel.

PART I: POTTERY IN THE ANCIENT WORLD

1. POTTERS AND POTTERY

a. *The Invention of Pottery*

The plastic qualities of clay were known to people for a long time before they started to produce fired pottery. At least as early as the Mesolithic period, some 120,000 years ago, people were shaping figurines of animals and human beings out of clay without firing them. The pre-pottery inhabitants of the site of Halicar in Anatolia built their houses of standardized clay bricks. This shows that a brickmaker's mould must have already been known to them. At the same time, some of the decorative techniques later used on pottery were in use long before fired pottery was made. Red slip and high polish were characteristic of clay floors and walls in pre-pottery Neolithic houses, while red-and-black-painted, decorated, unbaked clay figurines date from the same period. The invention of pottery occurred, therefore, only when people discovered the

role fire played in hardening the clay and causing it to retain its shape. It must be appreciated that the earliest potsherds discovered are the result of a long process of trial and error by many persons during long ages of time.

The invention of pottery lagged behind many other technological developments. While Stone Age people knew how to work stone, bone, and shell by grinding and drilling, and how to weave baskets and work leather, they knew nothing about firing pottery. The explanation for pottery's late appearance is probably related to the Stone Age life-style. These ancient people were nomadic hunters, and used permanent and unbreakable materials and developed the skills required to work them. Only when they settled down in agricultural communities could the cheap and easily workable clay take its place among other raw materials. In fact, it took their place to a large extent. It follows, then, that pottery is always connected with sedentary Neolithic communities. It is not, however,

The god Khnum forming people on a potter's wheel

always connected with the earliest stages of settled life. On the contrary, Neolithic people in many places were settled and practising agriculture for hundreds and even thousands of years without knowing how to make pottery. In some areas Neolithic people had advanced to such a state that they built towns fortified with huge walls and towers before they knew how to make pottery. It seems that economic and social development were more rapid than the successful adoption of clay as a material for vessels of everyday use.

How did the Neolithic people learn to fire their pots? Several suggestions have been offered to explain the accident, or possibly the deliberate search, that led to this invention, but there is still no decisive answer to the question. Excavation of Neolithic sites both in Jericho in Palestine and in Jarmo in the Kurdish foothills has brought to light a possible trend of events. The people of these sites used to coat the shallow pits in the floors of their houses with clay. In these pits, which were probably used for cooking, the fire hardened the clay and transformed it into a kind of fixed basin. This might have led the people to try to make clay vessels which were not attached to the pits. Another suggestion connecting cooking or baking with the idea of firing clay arises from the exca-

Unbaked clay animals

vations of the early Neolithic site of Catal Huyuk in Anatolia. There, a baking oven was found side by side with another kind of oven. In this second oven, there were two chambers which were separated by a wall. This installation, interpreted as a pottery kiln, might hint at a possible connection between cooking and firing the vessels.

Another trend of thought suggests that clay was used to seal reed baskets. This suggestion is based on the fact that stamps of reed mats were found on the floors of pre-pottery houses in Jericho. It is possible that a clay-coated basket fell into a fire and burned out, while the clay hardened into a vessel. An accident

of this kind might have triggered the process which finally brought about the invention of pottery as an independent craft.

It seems unlikely that pottery was invented in one place from which it later diffused far and wide. On the contrary, pottery is such a basic craft and its raw materials are so abundant that people in many places arrived at it independently.

Religions and cultures which had apparently no connections in early times, such as the Near East, the Far East, and the Americas, all practised pottery and developed their own styles and uses. Even within each region, there was probably more than one centre in which pottery was invented and developed.

The earliest known pottery was discovered in Anatolia, where pottery-bearing strata in the site of Catal Huyuk were dated to rather later than 7000 BC by the Carbon 14 method. But the new invention apparently did not succeed at first. It soon disappeared, to reappear only thousands of years later. At that time, it was technically improved to such an extent that it could take the place of wood or bone vessels. Only around the middle of the 5th millennium BC did pottery become more or less common. At that time, it was found in many village communities spread throughout the northern part of the Fertile Crescent, from the foothills of the Iranian Plateau to Syria and Palestine. Towards the end of that millennium, pottery vessels made their first appearance in Egypt. The Far East and the New World lagged behind the Near East: the earliest pottery in China dates to about 3000 BC, while that from Central and South America dates from about 1000 BC.

When investigating the technique and methods of ancient pottery-making, it is very useful to study primitive and traditional societies. Thus we can fill in gaps in our knowledge and understand the processes and instruments which have left their marks on ancient pots but which were not actually found in excavations of ancient sites. The following description is therefore partly based on actual ancient material, and partly on contemporary methods still practised in traditional societies.

The production of pottery is a production of several stages. The essential stages are preparing the clay, forming the pot, and firing it. An additional stage, not necessary to the actual making of pottery, but extremely common, is decoration. Methods of decorating pottery will be discussed in the following chapter. Here, we shall deal with those processes without which pottery cannot be made.

b. *The Potter's Role in Ancient Times*

We have no records describing the potter and his role in society in ancient days. But on this subject, too, one may draw analogies with traditional societies to reconstruct a picture of the past. It is possible that the early potters were the women of the villages, much like women in villages in Africa, Anatolia and Kurdistan, or in the Indian pueblos of the south-western United States today. The women produced hand-built pottery for household use as one of their many tasks, and were in no way specialized potters. However, side by side with the crude, home-made, hand-made pottery, excavations revealed fine-quality painted ware which was dispersed over wide areas. Such widely diffused pottery as, for example, the Halaf Ware dating from about 4500–4000 BC was popular all over northern Mesopotamia and Syria. To explain this phenomenon, an interesting speculation was proposed by Matson ("Ceramics Ecology" in *Ceramics and Man*). Matson argues that agricultural Semitic societies have always looked down upon artisans specializing in any kind of craft. The farmers themselves did not indulge in craftwork, but employed the services of specialized travelling artisans. Such was probably the case of the metal-working Kenites in biblical times, and the same is known today in many societies. In Ethiopia, a country in which ancient Semitic traditions are preserved to this day, the Falashas — a sect of black Jews — serve as travelling potters for the predominantly Christian population. Similarly, on the island of Crete, there are groups of potters who tour the island in the summer months and set up shop wherever there is sufficient clay, fuel, and water, as well as a large enough population to buy their products. In the winter months, these potters return to their villages and practise agriculture. It is possible that such was the status and way of life of professional potters in ancient days. "It is not impossible," concludes Matson (p. 212), "that the Samarra and Halaf styles owe their wide distribution to wandering tribes with craft specialization."

The introduction of the potter's wheel has brought about many changes in the potter's craft. Firstly, pottery became an exclusively male craft. Secondly, the introduction of the potter's wheel, which enabled the potter to produce at a great speed, has led to the industrialization of the potter's craft. Workshops were soon set up which produced large quantities of vessels. Standardized methods and techniques as well as uniformity of styles began to prevail. It would seem, however, that the village people continued to produce pottery by hand, and so we might find hand-built pots side by side with more sophisticated "industrial" vessels in the same ancient settlement.

The use of the potter's wheel, with its higher technical demands, seems to be related to the size and economic state of the community. Since only larger and more prosperous communities could afford the services of specialized craftsmen, it has been suggested that the introduction of the wheel is connected with the rise of urban centres.

The organization of highly developed workshops in urban centres is known from both literary and graphic sources from classical Greece. Some of these workshops were very large, employing

Youth decorating a kylix, Greek 5th century BC

up to 70 workers. They were, in fact, large enough to be called factories. The employees of these factories carried out all the stages of pottery making, from digging up the clay to firing the finished pots, except for painting them. Pottery painters were a class of their own, including women as well as men. It is interesting to note that in Athens, the potters, as well as other artisans and traders, were aliens with no citizenship rights.

Before the Archaic period in Greece‘ which started in the 7th century BC, pottery production showed conformity of shape and decoration with very little individuality. With the introduction of new firing and painting techniques, potters and painters began to develop distinct styles, and some of them, proud of their work, began to sign their pots with the formula: (X) made me (*m'epoisen* in Greek). At first, potter and painter were the same man, but from the middle of the 7th century BC, there was a clear distinction between the potter and the painter. The painter began to sign: (X) painted me (*m'egrapsen* in Greek). The earliest painters whom we know by name are Sophilos (590–570 BC) and Kleitian (570–550 BC). Some pottery painters had such a distinct style that, though their names are lost, their works can be clearly identified. Although the artistic achievements of many of the pottery painters were remarkable, they were considered artisans only, and were not admitted to the ranks of the painters.

The secret techniques of producing red and black gloss pottery which were developed in Greece were passed over to Rome, probably by Greek potters who were enslaved by the Romans. Their signatures, Greek names written in Latin characters, are quite often stamped on black gloss pottery produced in Roman factories.

2. HOW POTTERY IS MADE

a. *Clay*

Clay is the name given to fine particles produced by the gradual weathering of rock-forming minerals, particularly feldspar. Feldspar is the main mineral of granite and gneiss, the rocks which form about three-fourths of the surface of the earth. Clay, therefore, is one of the most common and widespread natural materials. The main agent of the weathering process is water, which grinds the rocks and dissolves the soluble minerals in them. The resulting clay is a finely granulated material composed mainly of alumina and silica (about 75 per cent) with small amounts of other

Clay producing soil

Chinese porcelain vase

minerals, especially iron oxide. Clay is characterized by the fineness of its grains. The average diameter of a particle of clay is one micron, which is one-thousandth of a millimetre. There are gradations of fineness in different types of clays, depending on the length of their exposure to the process of erosion. The fineness of the grains of clay, together with their small, flat, plate-like shape accounts for its plasticity, the most important quality for the production of pottery. As a rule, the finer the particles, the more plastic the clay.

The purest form of clay, composed of silica and alumina only, is called kaolin. This name is derived from a Chinese word meaning "high ridge", after the location where this material was found in China. Kaolin is a primary clay, which means that it was deposited near its parent rock and not transported to considerable distances. It is, therefore, not widely dispersed. But kaolin's relative scarcity and the fact that it requires very high firing temperatures to harden it into white, fine porcelain limited its use in ancient days. It was, however, known in China, where it was used as early as the 2nd century AD as a slip to coat clay vessels. It took the Chinese potters centuries to find large pure kaolin deposits and to refine their firing techniques before they started producing their famous translucent porcelain ware.

Since the 9th century AD, Chinese porcelains have been exported to the West, where they are greatly admired to this day.

Unlike kaolin, ordinary earthenware clays are secondary clays. They have been transported from their places of origin by water, wind, or ice. These clays, therefore, are found all over the earth's surface, except for sandy deserts and coral islands. They cover vast plains, lake beds, and river valleys. While they were on the move, earthenware clays absorbed different impurities which serve as fluxes and lower the range of temperatures required to fire them. These impurities, and especially iron oxide, are also responsible for the colour of the clay. While kaolin is pure white, earthenware has a colour range from yellow-buff to red-brown.

b. *Preparing the Clay*

Clay in its natural state is rarely fit for immediate use. It has to be ground and

Kneading clay

Series of shallow refining pits used by Arab potters

then sifted or suspended in water to remove all large and coarse particles. Different ingredients are added to the clay to improve its qualities. Sometimes the clay is not plastic enough and finer clay has to be added to increase the average plasticity. On the other hand, the clay might be so plastic that it hardly retains any shape. Such clay calls for the addition of coarser ingredients for balance. Non-plastic materials such as sand, gravel, ground-fired potsherds or cut straw are also added to the clay. These ingredients open the clay up and allow the water to evaporate more freely. This helps reduce excessive shrinkage, secures even drying, and lessens the risk of cracking. The clay is then well wedged, often by stamping with the feet, to get an even mixture of all the ingredients with water. The clay is left to soak in water in a descending series of shallow pits. The solution flows slowly from pit to pit, while the coarse particles sink to the bottom of the pits. The fine solution which reaches the lowest pit is dried in the sun and ready for use. The clay is then wedged again to get all the air bubbles out of it and to bring it to the right consistency. Experienced potters do not use newly prepared clay. They prefer to store it and let it age. Ageing the clay increases its workability, both by assuring that each tiny particle of clay gets thoroughly moistened and by letting organic compounds develop in the clay. Traditional potters in Japan used to

Japanese potter kneading clay with his feet

store their clay from generation to generation: a potter would use clay prepared by his father.

c. *Forming the Vessel*

When the clay is ready, the potter proceeds to form his vessel. He can choose one of several ways of shaping a pot. A combination of more than one technique is also possible.

Direct shaping or pinching is undoubtedly the simplest technique. The potter holds a lump of clay in the palm of one hand and shapes it with the other. This technique, which needs no utensils at all, was most probably the first technique used by the earliest potters. Direct shaping is greatly appreciated in cultures which strive towards simplicity and austerity of form and try to capture the spontaneous beauty of nature. Japanese potters producing cups for the Tea Ceremony masters have created some of the most beautiful pottery in this simple way.

While small bowls and cups are easily formed by direct shaping, large and complicated shapes are better suited to the technique of coil construction. Usually the potter starts his pot by forming the base. He then rolls the clay into even coils which he joins one on top of the other. In this way, he gradually builds up the walls of the pot. By apply-

Above and opposite: A Japanese potter forming small bowls with her elbow

ing bigger or smaller coils, the potter can narrow or widen his pot, and achieve more complicated forms than possible by direct shaping. There are practically no technical restrictions on the potter who forms his pot with coils. He can create the most fantastic shapes. Coil construction was the most common technique of all pottery-producing people prior to the invention and spread of the potter's wheel.

The use of moulds for forming pottery is also an extremely old technique. The earliest moulds were probably vessels made of other materials, such as baskets, parts of gourds, or skin receptacles. The potter spreads his clay either inside or on the outside of the mould and thus easily copies its shape. The Pueblo Indians of the south-western United States to this day form the lower part of their pots inside a gourd and finish the upper

Arab potter coiling a pot on a straw mat

beautifully decorated with scenes in relief of people, animals, plants and geometric shapes, is the so-called "Arretine Ware" which enjoyed great popularity in the Roman Empire between 30 BC and AD 30. Arretine Ware was produced in factories in Italy and required great skill. The potter first prepared his mould by forming a hemispherical clay bowl which was the basic shape of his vessels.

part with coils. The advantages of the mould are particularly noted for mass-producing pottery with decorations in relief. A distinct class of moulded pottery,

Jar in the form of a bird, New Mexico, AD 1100–1300

Vessel in the shape of a man's head, Jericho, 1750–1550 BC

He then stamped the inside of this mould with a variety of decorated clay stamps prepared beforehand and available in the workshop. The spacing and combination of the design depended on the taste and sense of composition of the potter. The mould was then fired and ready for use. When the potter wanted to shape a vessel, he would press wet clay into the fired mould and the decorations would appear in the positive. Forming the interior and the rim of the vessel and adding a foot and handles would complete the process.

Moulds were used to produce a variety of objects or parts of objects characterized by detailed plastic decorations. Oil lamps and small statuettes used for household cults were the most common clay objects manufactured in moulds.

Right: Arretine bowl from Capua, 1st century BC

Below: Mould for Arretine vases, signed by Pilemo, late 1st century BC

Potter's wheel found at Hazor, 1450–1250 BC

d. *The Potter's Wheel*

The potter who works with coils usually forms his pot on some supporting base such as a piece of wood, a slab of stone, or a mat. By turning the pot on this base during the process of shaping, the potter can sit in one spot and better control all sides of the pot. This is especially important when producing large vessels. Stamped mats on the bases of jars dating from around 3500 BC indicate that this process is extremely old. The method of thus turning the vessel raises the interesting question if it already contains in it the seeds of the idea of the potter's wheel. There is,

however, a crucial difference between rotating the pot on a base and forming it on a wheel. The speed of rotation which the wheel builds up creates centrifugal forces which throw the lump of clay, while the potter has to control it and force it to maintain the shape he wants. A wheel has to spin at least 100 revolutions per minute to create centrifugal forces. A base, on the other hand, cannot develop any speed of its own and the potter builds his pot gradually by adding coils.

We do not know what stages existed between the use of a turned base and the invention of the rotating potter's wheel. We do have evidence, however, of a

A contemporary Arab potter working a foot-powered potter's wheel

Making huge pots on the potter's wheel, Japan, contemporary

A wooden model of a potter's workshop, Egypt, 21st century BC

primitive wheel, probably no more than a base with a pivot. This device, called a turntable or a tournette, has left its marks on the walls and rims of small bowls dating from the second half of the 4th millennium BC. While fine concentric lines testify that these small bowls were slowly rotated, probably to obtain a finer finish, it is certain that the speed of rotation was not enough to create the whole vessel.

The earliest real potter's wheel actually found in excavations in the Ancient Near East comes from the town of Ur in Sumer and is dated to the second half of the 4th millennium BC. The ancient wheels were made of two flat round slabs, usually of stone but some-

times also of baked clay. One had a hole in its centre and the other had a pivot fitting exactly into the hole. Contemporary potters who tried to operate ancient wheels soon found out that they do not work. The rotary movement stopped the minute the potter started to press down his lump of clay on the upper stone of the wheel and centre it. It does not seem likely that an apprentice could keep the wheel rotating since the stones are very small and could accommodate only one pair of hands — the potter's. It was therefore suggested that a large slab of wood, about two feet in diameter, was fastened to the upper stone. This enlarged working area allowed space for the hands of an apprentice who would keep

·otating the wheel and create a suitable
momentum for the potter to centre the
:lay and create the vessels. A wheel that
was thus reconstructed proved to be useful and a series of vessels was actually
thrown on it.

The early potter certainly had to use
some lubricant, such as oil, fat, or
bitumen to reduce the friction of the
wheel and make the rotation easier.
Although this type of wheel is very primitive, it did not change for thousands of
years, until the invention of a wheel
rotated by the foot. The foot wheel was a
great step forward since it freed both
hands for forming the pot. It is not
known when and where the foot wheel
was invented, but it was probably not
known before the Hellenistic period
(2nd century BC). The primitive hand
wheel, however, did not prevent the
ancient potter from forming some of the
most beautiful pottery that was ever
created. It is interesting to note the
suggestion of Gordon Childe (*A History
of Technology*, Oxford 1955, pp. 200–202),
based on an analogy with a wheel used by
contemporary Arab potters in Palestine,
that the two slabs just described as the
wheel itself are actually the bearings for a
foot wheel which was made of wood.
Childe assumes, therefore, that foot
wheels were known and used as early as
the 4th millennium BC.

The potter's wheel, or rather the knowl-

One of the jars in which the Dead Sea Scrolls
were found, 1st century AD

edge of centrifugal force and its application for pottery-making, diffused slowly from Mesopotamia both eastward and westward.

The pre-Colombian cultures of the Americas did not know the wheel at all, and their magnificent pottery was hand-built. In some outstanding instances the introduction of the potter's wheel did not altogether replace earlier techniques. The inhabitants of the island of Cyprus, for example, though they produced their household pottery on the wheel in the 2nd millennium BC, nevertheless exported large quantities of beautiful and technically excellent hand-built pottery all over the Near East.

e. Combined Methods

Both in ancient and in modern times, pottery was sometimes produced by combining two methods. The typical pottery that was produced in Syria and Palestine during the last centuries of the 3rd millennium and the first centuries of the 2nd millennium BC combined throwing and coiling. The bodies of the vessels — jars, bottles and teapots — were coiled and clearly exhibit irregularities in shape and an uneven surface. Sometimes the joints between the coils are felt. The neck and rim, however, were thrown on a wheel. The two parts were joined when they were leather-hard,

and the joint was disguised by rows of incised lines. It is hard to tell why this method was used. It is probably not because the potter's wheel was too slow. On the contrary, the necks and rims are finely shaped and testify to the existence and use of a fast wheel. Interestingly small vessels which could easily be made entirely on the wheel were also produced in this combined fashion. Is it because of specialization in the potter's workshop, where the less skilled workers would coil the bodies and the master potter would throw the necks and rims? We have no evidence for this assumption, although it might be possible.

Many traditional societies today in Mediterranean and Middle Eastern countries produce their pottery in the same manner. The potters of the village of Beit Shebab in the Lebanon form the bodies of their jars and bottles out of thick coils of clay. Then they beat the clay with a wooden beater while supporting the wall from the inside against a wooden disc. This beating raises the walls of the vessel, thins them, strengthens them, and gives the vessel its final shape. The body of the vessel is then placed on the wheel, and a neck, prepared on the wheel beforehand, is attached to it. The joint is smoothed on the wheel and the rim is shaped and finished. This method, preserved by hereditary families of potters with strong traditions, is probably a survival of methods used in the area in very ancient times. Traditional skills seem to resist both changes of population and modern innovations.

f. *Firing the Clay Vessels*

Up until the time of firing, the potter was free to shape his clay by whichever method and form he pleased. The clay was soft and yielded to his touch. Now comes the moment when the pot is trusted to the fire which fixes its form and makes it suitable for use. The fire reveals all the flaws of the pot, such as air bubbles trapped in its walls, or faulty connections between the coils. A badly formed pot, or one which was not dry enough before firing, might even explode and break the entire load of the kiln. Firing is, therefore, a crucial stage in the process of making pottery.

Before being put in the fire, a clay vessel has to be left to dry. While drying, it loses part of its water and shrinks by about ten per cent. If the vessel does not dry slowly and evenly, it may warp and crack. When the vessel is dry, it can be

Firing pottery vessels in a primitive kiln

handled, but it is extremely fragile and has to be kept away from water.

Great changes occur in the clay when it is fired. At first, all the water added to the clay while preparing it evaporates and the vessel dries completely. This process requires about 350°C of heat. At this temperature, the chemical water, locked in its molecular structure, starts leaving the clay. At about 500°C, the clay loses most of its plasticity and will not disintegrate any more. Another change that occurs in the kiln is the oxidation of the inorganic and organic matter included in the clay, especially carbon. Complete oxidation occurs at about 900°C. If the kiln cannot reach this temperature, or if there is not enough oxygen in the kiln, the carbon will remain and blacken the clay.

The earliest kiln was probably no more than an open bonfire. The pots could have been piled on the ground or in a shallow pit and covered with fuel such as dry branches or animal dung. Such a firing can last as little as an hour, but breakage might be considerable because of uneven heating. The pile of pots can be covered with earth and the heat is retained better and more evenly. An open fire can produce temperatures up to 750–800°C, which is sufficient to fire earthenware vessels. But the vessels thus fired will be black because of the smoke.

The earliest potsherds found are black, soft, and porous. This indicates that they were probably fired in an open fire. They were possibly coated after the firing with animal fat to enable them to hold water. After a relatively short period, however, the Neolithic people started producing pottery decorated with coloured slip and paint. This shows that the method of firing has advanced to such a degree that the potter could control the atmosphere of the firing and eliminate the effects of the smoke. It would seem that these early potters had already invented an actual kiln. Even the most primitive kiln requires two separate chambers, one for the pots and one for the fire. Good ventilation is essential, as well, to secure a continuous high fire and to maintain an oxidizing atmosphere in the kiln chamber. Once invented, the basic form of the kiln was not changed for many centuries.

The earliest pottery kiln to be discovered in Palestine dates to the 3rd millennium BC. It is a round structure with two storeys. The lower, with a central pillar supporting its roof, is the fire chamber. The pots are placed in the upper chamber, which has large holes in its floor to enable the heat to flow in. Such kilns can reach temperatures up to about 1,000°C. They can successfully fire all earthenware clays. Tests made on pottery vessels unearthed at Tel Beit Mirsim in Palestine, which date from the

2nd and 1st millennia BC, established firing temperatures for most of the pottery at less than 890°C. The highest temperature, 1,030°C, was recorded in vessels imported from Mycenae in Greece.

3. FORM AND DESIGN

a. *Form*

When the early potter started to produce his wares, he had a wide variety of natural and man-made containers from different materials to suggest shapes to him. These included gourds, ostrich eggs, hollowed wood, stone bowls, reed baskets, and leather bags. He did not have to invent new shapes. He only had to adapt the existing ones for his new material. Clay, by its very nature, can take almost any shape, and is therefore an ideal material for creating substitutes for any other material and shape. Many forms of ancient pottery clearly tried to imitate shapes made of other materials. Decorative techniques were developed to reproduce the surface qualities and textures of these materials onto pottery. Incisions and paint came to create an illusion of the quality of wood and stone or of the rows of weaving in basketry and stitches in sewn leather. Later, when metals were discovered and used for producing vessels, clay became the poor

Pottery vessels

man's substitute for the expensive gold, silver, and bronze vessels. Since the technical possibilities of metal are totally different from those of clay, the potter was confronted with such features as sharp angles, and thin, band-shaped handles. The fact that potters have succeeded, to a surprising extent, in copying these features shows the almost endless possibilities of clay as well as the high technical ability of the ancient craftsmen.

Left: Loading vessels in the kiln. Vessels are placed upside-down. The opening is blocked with mud. Contemporary Arab work

Above: Clay sauceboat or drinking cup, Greece *ca.* 2000 BC

West Kennet beaker, 2000–1000 BC

It is hard to argue for the existence of forms inherent in the nature of clay as a raw material, since clay seems to be the one material that can take on any shape. Even the round forms so commonly associated with pottery are more a matter of tradition and techniques of forming — especially the use of the wheel — rather than forms which spring out of the innate character of the clay. Ovoid and rectangular shapes are as successful as round shapes. The prevalence of vessels made in

Right: A Philistine jug

Overleaf left: A Philistine krater

Overleaf right: Phoenician pottery — mask and burnished jugs

Left: Mesopotamian polychrome plate   *Above:* Coiled vessel from the Congo

Red-Figured Rhyton (drinking cup) in the shape
of a bull's head, Athenian, *ca.* 460 BC

the shape of human beings or animals in all periods and all cultures further illustrates this point. These vessels, either realistic or abstract in concept, show the unlimited ability of creating forms in clay.

b. *Decoration*

The same is true of decorative techniques, as almost any possible kind of decoration can be adapted to pottery. The potter can incise, comb, stamp, add relief, or cut away sections of his pot. He can also paint, slip, burnish, or glaze it. All of these techniques were well known and freely used in antiquity. Their application fluctuates with the technical ability and the taste of the period. For a while, one technique may win great popularity, only to dwindle and give way to another. These decorative elements are therefore very important in identifying a culture, appreciating and evaluating its artistic level, and learning the tastes of its people.

Of all the decorative techniques, painting was the most common. The surface of the vessel has always offered an attractive background for the imagination of the potter, who created a variety of designs ranging from the simplest geometric lines through realistic or fantastic figures and most sophisticated scenes. It seems that in a very early age, in the 5th to 4th millennia BC, there were two Near Eastern centres in which pottery painting flourished. These were the hilly regions of Anatolia and Iran, and from there the painting techniques spread to the lowlands.

The significance of paintings on pottery lies also in the fact that very often they are the only traces left from rich traditions of painting in many ancient cultures, such as Greece, Mesopotamia, Syria, and Palestine where paintings or frescoes did not survive. We know for certain that the painting on Greek vases is but a faint echo of the beautiful fresco work which adorned public buildings in Athens and of which nothing has remained.

Although many techniques are purely decorative, others, which greatly enhance the beauty of the vessel, also increase its usability, especially by making it more waterproof. Slipping and burnishing are techniques with these double qualities. It seems, however, that the early potters were mainly concerned with the aesthetic qualities of these techniques. In fact, they usually confined the slip and burnish to the better, more elegant vessels, and did not use them on everyday vessels such as water jars or cooking pots which certainly required as much waterproofing as possible. The third and most successful technique for waterproofing a vessel is glazing. Although glazing was

Cretan jug with grass design, 1450–1250 BC

discovered in the Near East at a very early age, it did not enjoy great popularity in the ancient world. Almost every kind of decoration is applied to the pot before it is fired, when it is semi-dry and in the state of being leather-hard.

c. *Slip*

Slip is a coat of thin clay applied to the surface of the pot before it is fired. Slip is a solution of water and the finest particles of the same clay from which the vessel is made. It is better, however, to use slip made from finer and better clay. The potter may dip his pot several times in the slip, or paint the slip on with a mop or a thick brush. The aesthetic qualities of the slip lie in the uniformity of the surface thus achieved and in the fact that, due to the firmness of the particles, the colour of the slip is deeper than that of the clay. The difference in colour between body and slip must have been used to create pleasing contrasts by painting slip on parts of the pot only, or by scratching through the coat of slip to reveal the clay underneath.

The most splendid examples of masterly application of slip, combined with absolute knowledge of firing processes, are the Black Figured and Red Figured wares produced in Athens in the 6th and 5th centuries BC. For centuries, the methods by which the Greek potters obtained the fine shiny black and red colours of their pottery was totally unknown. Modern research proved that the colours were not obtained from different pigments, but from the same slip, which changed colours in different atmospheres of firing created in the kiln by masterly handling of the firing process. The Greek potter prepared a slip of the finest particles of the same clay he used to make his pots. A weak solution of this slip was first applied to the entire surface of the unfired pot. When this coat dried, the painter painted the design on with a more concentrated slip. Since the normal clay found in the vicinity of Athens contains a large amount of iron (up to 17 per cent of the composition of the clay), its colour after firing in an oxidizing atmosphere is red. If, however, the potter closed his kiln and shut off his supply of oxygen, the carbon monoxide formed in the kiln would cause the iron to turn black. The first stage of firing the figured Greek vases was an oxidizing fire. The entire pot turned red, deeper red where the slip was more concentrated. Then ventilation was shut off, and in the reducing atmosphere the pot turned black. The third stage was the most critical. The closed vents were re-opened to admit enough oxygen to turn the thinly slipped areas of the pot red again. Those parts of the pot which were coated with thicker slip remained black.

A two-spouted highly burnished jar, Peru, *ca.* AD 500

d. *Burnishing and Glazing*

Burnishing means polishing the surface of the pot with the aid of a pebble, a piece of wood, or another hard and smooth material before the pot is fired. When fired, the burnished parts of the vessel obtain a gloss. An entirely burnished pot has an overall beautiful gloss. The burnishing consolidates the clay particles and thus improves the pot's ability to retain water. Burnish and slip are usually applied together to the same pot, and the combination of the two is most pleasing. Burnishing seems to be the oldest known decorative technique, and it is found on some of the earliest Neolithic pottery known as "dark-faced burnished ware". Burnishing has been and still is popular wherever glazing did not develop. Outstanding pieces of slipped and burnished pottery are the sculptural vessels of the pre-Columbian cultures of the Americas.

A glaze is a thin glossy coat which is melted onto the surface of the pot by heating. Basically, glaze is composed of the same minerals as clay — silica and alumina. Therefore, if a vessel is fired to a high temperature, the clay will start to melt and form a rough coat of glaze on its surface. To lower the melting point and adjust it to the normal temperature required for firing the vessel, different fluxes are added to the alumina and silica. Two kinds of fluxes are most suitable for the relatively low temperatures at which earthenware is fired. The two are alkalines, such as soda or borax, and lead. Both alkaline and lead glazes were invented in antiquity in the ancient Near East and from there spread westward to Europe and eastward as far as China and Japan. Although glazing became the most common pottery decoration from the Middle Ages on, it enjoyed only limited popularity in its homeland in antiquity.

Glaze was probably known in Egypt as early as the 5th millennium BC. This early glaze was alkaline, based on soda which is found in a natural state in the deserts surrounding Egypt. Soda probably got accidentally mixed with clay from which beads, small sculptures, and ornamental pieces were fashioned. When fired, the soda is drawn to the surface of the object and forms a glaze. The Egyptians also discovered early that addition of copper minerals, most probably malachite which was used as eye paint, produced brilliant turquoise and blue colours in the glaze. This accidental discovery was soon understood by the Egyptians, who started producing their famous "faience" objects from a mixture of clay, powdered quartz, soda, and

copper. Later, other oxides were tried, producing such colours as cobalt blue, manganese black, chrome yellow and red, and others. The term "faience", however, is misleading. This name derives from Faenza, an important pottery producing centre in Italy during the Renaissance, whose glazed products were copied in France in the 16th to 18th centuries. When French archaeologists first discovered Egyptian glazed objects, they wrongly thought that they were similar to the glazed objects they knew in France, and so they named them "faience".

The faience body, high in silica, was not plastic. This made it suitable only for producing small objects in moulds. A great improvement came when the Egyptians discovered how to apply the glaze materials to the surface of the object rather than mix them into the clay. As a result, they could produce glazed clay vessels of any shape. The use of alkaline glazes continued in the Hellenistic and Roman periods and later in some of the magnificent Moslem pottery. Their place, however was gradually taken over by lead glazes, which are easier to prepare and apply.

It is assumed that lead glazes were invented in Babylonia or Syria, some time in the 2nd millennium BC. Lead, in the form of galena which is the natural lead compound, is quite abundant in

Anatolia. It was discovered at quite an early age that it melts at a low temperature and forms a glaze. The composition of lead glazes is much simpler than alkaline glazes. Actually, one can simply dust powdered galena on a damp pot and get a fairly good glaze after firing. This method was commonly practised in medieval Europe. As with alkaline glazes, a wide variety of colours is obtained by addition of different metallic oxides.

Some time in the last quarter of the 2nd millennium, the Assyrians discovered that addition of tin greatly enhances the stability of the lead glaze colours. From then on, they started to decorate the walls of temples and palaces with polychrome glazed tiles. The most splendid examples which have survived are the gigantic animal friezes which decorate the procession street, the Gate of Ishtar, and the throne room in the palace of King Nebuchadnezzar (605–562 BC) in his capital city Babylon. The knowledge of lead glazes spread eastward to China, where the earliest examples date to about 500 BC.

1. THE IMPORTANCE OF POTTERY TO ARCHAEOLOGICAL INVESTIGATIONS

It has long been recognized that pottery is one of the archaeologist's most valuable tools for studying the past. Pottery is particularly important when historical documents are rare and interpretation has to be based exclusively on material finds. Pottery vessels were probably the most common utensils in ancient times, used equally in palaces and in humble dwellings, serving the living and the dead. They are therefore found in profusion in every site which was once occupied, and are undoubtedly the most common type of finds in any excavation. The vast number of pottery vessels in every ancient site is also due to the nature of the fired clay. Even if buried for thousands of years, pottery will not disintegrate or rot, while almost every other material will be greatly damaged or disappear altogether under the same conditions. This fact brings about a great

increase in the proportion of clay objects as against objects of any other material far beyond that which had existed originally. Although we know hardly anything about the fashions of furniture or clothing of ancient people, we can record with great detail the minute changes which have occurred in the style of pottery. Both the form and decoration of pottery vessels change relatively frequently as a result of change in the taste of the potters or the customers, or technical improvements, or of influences from different cultural areas. Tracing these fluctuations is a fascinating study in continuity and change, innovation and diffusion. Chemists and physicists now help the archaeologist with modern techniques and instruments which help trace the origin of clay and thus determine the place where the vessels were made. These examinations are of particular significance, since styles can diffuse in various ways. They can be brought along by travelling potters, by exporting activities, or by settlers who leave their homeland and move to a new region where they continue to produce pottery in the fashion they remembered from their previous homes. Pottery, therefore, is a most sensitive barometer, helping the archaeologist evaluate the technical and aesthetic achievements of the culture he studies. It allows him to identify trade relations, foreign influence, war and conquest, and population movements. Moreover, pottery is an invaluable tool of the establishment of chronological order. All of these aspects of the place of pottery in archaeological research are eloquently, though with some exaggeration, described by Professor Myers in *Cambridge Ancient History* (1920, pp. 70–1):

> The utter uselessness of pottery, once broken . . . is the main cause of its archaeological value: for where broken pottery is cast out of a settlement, there it is allowed to lie and accumulate, layer over layer, later over earlier: so that the "sequence dating" derived from such a rubbish heap is as secure as the sequence of the fossils in the sedimentary rocks, and of the highest value as evidence for change of style, that is to say, of the notions, industrial and aesthetic, of successive generations of makers and breakers of pottery. As breakage and replacement are constant, clay almost ubiquitous, and pot-transport risky,

the pottery series in any settlement is exceptionally continuous and coherent: the smallest changes in style are recorded infallibly, directly, and immediately, and every older object cast upon the same waste-heap is conserved automatically in stratified order, and can be dated by the potsherds around it, between older ones below and later ones above.

2. DAY TO DAY USE OF POTTERY

Let us now enter the house of a person who lived many years ago. Let us inspect the pottery vessels found in the kitchen and other rooms of the house, and try to understand in what way and for what purpose the housewife used them. Of course, we must remember that the vessels were not found intact and neatly arranged in shelves. On the contrary, ancient houses were destroyed a long time ago. Their roofs and walls collapsed, and the easily breakable pottery vessels were discovered shattered to pieces and scattered all over the floors of the rooms. During the process of excavation, the sherds were carefully collected, and the vessels were then labouriously reconstructed. Often, however, parts of vessels are missing and sometimes just one sherd remained from the whole vessel.

Two houses excavated in the flourishing town of Hazor inhabited in the first half of the 8th century BC by Israelite families were chosen for this survey. In one house, a jar with a Hebrew inscription incised on its body was found. The inscription, composed of the letters L M K B R M in the ancient Hebrew script, was interpreted as "belonging to Makhbiram" — Makhbiram being the name of the owner of the jar, who undoubtedly lived in this house. Thus we can get acquainted with Mr Makhbiram and his next-door neighbour.

The two houses were built side by side, with a common wall between them. They were rather small — one had two rooms and the other had three rooms. Each house had a small, open courtyard. The entrance to each house was through a shop which opened to the street. We can therefore suppose that Mr Makhbiram and his neighbours were shop-keepers, and that their houses represent average dwellings of the citizens of Hazor, probably not poor, but certainly not of the wealthy class. The pottery repertoire found in them can therefore give an accurate picture of the storing, cooking, and serving vessels at the disposal of an average ancient housewife.

The pottery ensemble is quite wide, and the housewives had many different vessels at their disposal. Bowls, undoubtedly used for eating, were very common. Fourteen different bowls were recorded

by the excavators. Six of the bowls were small, deep and angular in profile. Two had straight flaring walls, while the other six were large and rounded and had a thick lip. It is interesting to note that the ancient household did not have a flat plate, so common in our kitchens. Also missing is a drinking cup. Its function was filled, instead, by the small, deep bowls.

The ancient housewives cooked dinner for the family in pottery cooking pots. All ten pots found in the two houses are similarly shaped. They are medium-sized, closed, and often have two handles. The pots are all made of coarse hard clay and often have soot and smoke patches on the outside. There is no vessel which can be identified as a lid. If these pots were covered during cooking, the straight-sided bowls might have served this purpose. The stove on which the housewife cooked was of simple construction, sometimes made of earth and sometimes of pottery sherds. The stove found in one of the rooms, undoubtedly the kitchen, was made of the upper part of a broken jar, placed upside down on the earth floor and surrounded by a circle of small stones. The pot could be securely placed on this crude stand, while the fire would be burning underneath.

The kraters — large, deep, two-handled vessels — were used for preparing food. Since the five kraters found in the houses had no patches of smoke, it is obvious that the housewives did not use them for actual cooking but rather for mixing dough or salads or for serving large quantities of food to their families.

Liquids were served in jugs. Common to the period were decanters, which undoubtedly ranked among the best products of the Israelite potters. The five decanters found in the Hazor houses were used for cooling and serving water, much like the *jara*, a similar Arab vessel used today. Wine was probably served in globular jugs. These often had a pinched trefoil lip which facilitated pouring. Only one jug was found in each household. In one of the houses, a fragment of an imported Cypro-Phoenician decorated jug was also found.

One flask — a round, flat, vessel with a rounded base and two handles — was discovered. This vessel, which cannot stand, was designed for carrying a drink, much like a modern water canteen. It may indicate that someone in the house was preparing to take a journey.

The most common vessels in the Hazor households were storage jars. Sixteen different two-handled jars are mentioned by the excavators. The jars are of two basic shapes. One type has a long cylindrical body ending in a point, and its shoulders are sharply angular.

Various types of pottery vessels from Makhbiram's house, found at Hazor.

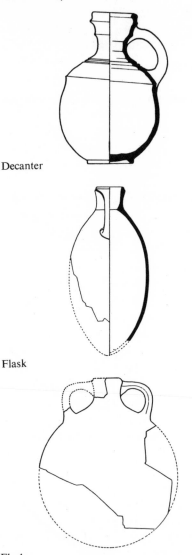

Decanter

Flask

Flask

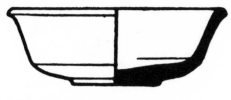

Small bowl

Bowl with straight walls

Large rounded bowl

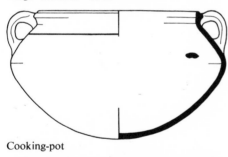

Cooking-pot

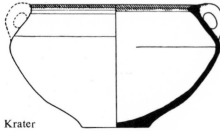

Krater

These jars came in two sizes. The small one was about 40–45 centimetres long, and the large ones were 70–80 centimetres long. The second type of jar has an oval body with sloping shoulders on a rounded bottom. Both types of jar could not stand by themselves. They were probably placed in shallow holes in the earth floors of the rooms, and were leaned against the wall. The jar in one kitchen were discovered in groups. Five cylindrical jars were found in the corner of a room, and four oval ones were in another corner of the same room. One of the oval jars bore two Hebrew inscriptions.

One unusual jar has a perforated spout. It is commonly thought that this kind of spout served as a holder for the smaller dipper juglet used to draw the liquid out of the jar. Through the holes in the bottom of the spout, the liquid which remained on the body of the juglet would drip back into the jar. This arrangement, meant for collecting every drop, indicates that the jar contained some expensive liquid — oil or wine most probably. It is hard to decide what the other jars contained, but their two distinct shapes indicate two different contents — probably liquids. One large jar, known as a *pithos*, was found. This was used for a large quantity of dry foodstuff — probably grain.

Eight dipper juglets were also found in the Hazor houses. Their bodies are cylindrical, ending in a round base. They have one handle and sometimes a pinched lip. These rather coarse juglets stand in contrast to the two sherds of fine, black juglets which have a round body and a pointed base. These black juglets may have contained cosmetic oil or some other luxury substance.

Only three pottery oil lamps were found in the two houses. These few lamps were certainly not enough to light the houses. Unless torches were used, and we have no evidence left of that, we have to assume that the inhabitants of these houses, and of all households of the period, went to bed early in the evening as soon as it turned dark. The oil lamps were simple bowls, and were pinched on one side to create a spout. The wick which floated on the oil that filled the bowl was secured in the spout.

In the courtyard of the Makhbiram's house, sherds of a large pottery basin were found. It is commonly thought that this basin served for washing before entering the house. Our ancient friend Mrs Makhbiram clearly tried to keep her family clean and orderly.

All the pottery vessels discovered in the two Hazor houses are well designed and functional, but they are not decorated. Only rarely were the common vessels decorated. This may reflect the austerity of life in ancient times, when ornamenta-

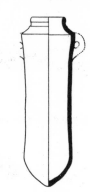

Cylindrical jar

Oval jar

Jar with perforated spout

Juglet

Juglet

Oil lamp

Side view of the oil lamp

tion of everyday objects seems to have been superfluous. Pottery vessels which were more artistically designed and decorated usually won international popularity and were widely traded. The only decorated sherd in the two Hazor houses is a piece of an imported Cypro-Phoenician jug.

Some tools and objects of other materials were also found in the two Hazor houses. They include basalt-stone bowls which served as mortars and their pestles, a few basalt millstones, an iron knife, some other unidentified iron tools, and an ivory cosmetic spoon.

The pottery ensembles of the two Israelite housewives who lived in Hazor were very similar, and fulfill the basic needs of the ancient household. As the basic needs of people hardly changed, pottery vessels for storing, cooking and serving food were present in every household of every culture and period, from the time pottery was invented in the Neolithic period to the time when other materials — glass, metal, plastic — started to replace it. Any layer excavated will therefore produce quantities of jars, bowls, cooking pots, jugs, and juglets. The style of these vessels, however, did change from place to place and from period to period. The importance of these changes to archaeological research will be dealt with in the following chapters.

3. INTERPRETING CHANGES IN POTTERY

Many aspects of archaeological investigation are based on the fact that pottery styles change. There are many reasons for these changes: gradual changes in taste, technical improvements, and influences from different cultural areas, either by movement of population or by trade.

Of course, pottery vessels are not the only artefacts that change. Architectural styles, functions of various buildings, and the whole concept of settlement designs change too. But many population groups did not build permanent settlements and maintained a nomadic way of life. Architectural elements, therefore, play no part in their culture and cannot be used to detect changes. Weapons, metal utensils, garments and furniture, for example, were used just as widely as pottery, and likewise underwent changes in style. But, unfortunately, most of these materials did not survive to tell their story. Pottery vessels remain, therefore, our best source for detecting changes and investigating their origin and meaning. By so doing, archaeologists can often reconstruct the course of events in a certain region, and thus arrive at a deeper understanding of the culture being investigated. Some suggested interpretations of changes that occurred in pottery groups will be presented in the following pages. All the examples are taken from the sphere of Palestinian archaeology.

a. *Gradual Transitions*

We are all aware of changes that occur in artefacts we use in everyday life. The clothes we wear, the furniture we use, the books we read, all change their designs rapidly. A contemporary car is quite different from a car produced just a few years ago. Almost everyone can point at a car and say, "This car is an early 1950s model." But in ancient times, the changes in styles were not as swift as they are today. Nevertheless, changes did occur, often simply to satisfy the people's imbedded desire for change.

A clear illustration of the gradual transition of this nature is found in the Palestinian pottery of the 2nd millennium BC. The illustration on the opposite page shows the gradual changes which took place in pottery vessels during the 2nd millennium BC.

These gradual changes in the shapes of pottery vessels prove that there were no drastic transitions in the population composition of the country. The 13th century people created their pottery in centuries-old traditions which they had inherited from their ancestors. This stability of population continued despite the rather drastic changes of the political scene.

Profile of pottery vessels of the 2nd millennium BC illustrating gradual changes in shape

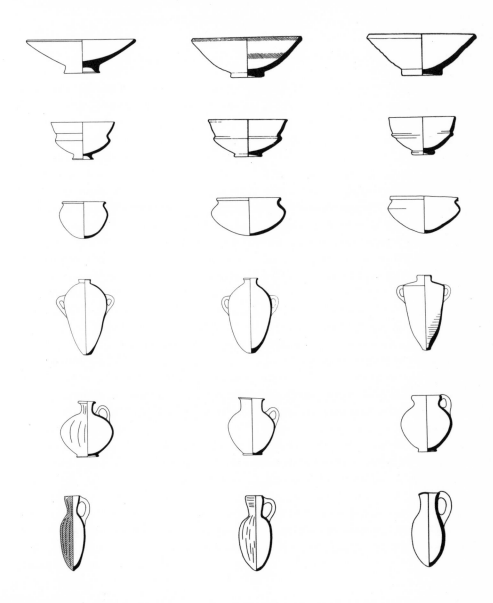

While the 17th-century people were ruled by the Hyksos — warriors of northern origin who took over both Palestine and Egypt — the people of the 15th and 13th centuries BC lived under Egyptian rule.

b. *Abrupt Changes*

While a gradual change in styles of pottery reflects the existence of a stable population striving for change for its own sake, sudden and drastic changes are a sure sign of major events such as the influx of a new population group with a different tradition of pottery production, or the destruction of one culture and its replacement by another.

The history of Palestinian pottery abounds with instances of drastic changes. Every few hundred years the pottery of the country changed completely, thus indicating the unstable nature of its population. New tribes were constantly entering the country, sometimes destroying the previous population and sometimes mixing with it.

The three examples which follow illustrate different aspects of interpreting events of this nature by the pottery which the involved populations used and left behind. Each example illuminates a different angle of the problem of pottery interpretation.

4. POTTERY AND HISTORY

a. *Pottery Complementing Historical Data*

The Philistines are a tribe of people who are quite well known. Both the Bible and Egyptian literary and graphic sources give us many details about them. They tell us that the Philistines originated in the islands of the Aegean Sea, that they invaded the Eastern Mediterranean regions both by land and by sea routes, that they were met in battle by the Egyptian army, and that they finally settled in the southern coastal plain of Palestine. These events took place in the late part of the 13th century BC and in the beginning of the 12th century BC. Incidentally, the name Palestine derives from these invading Philistines.

With all these facts well known, archaeological finds and especially pottery do not have the value of being the primary source for the study of the Philistines. The Philistine pottery instead reflects, in an interesting and lively way, the origin of these people, the stations along the routes of their wanderings, and their final assimilation into the local population.

Since historical sources tell us that the Philistines originated in the area of the Aegean Sea, it is not surprising that their pottery reflects Aegean, and particularly Mycenaean, shapes and decorations.

Philistine stirrup jar, both shape and decoration reflect Mycenaean tradition, 12th century BC

Philistine "beerjug". Note strainer in spout, 12th century BC

Of clear Mycenaean origin are bowls, large kraters, stirrup jars and spouted jugs and a strainer nicknamed beerjugs. These are all clearly different from the local pottery types. Into this basically Mycenaean repertoire, the Philistines incorporated at least one type of jug of typical Egyptian shape, and a bottle and horn-shaped vessel which are Cypriot in origin. These shapes were undoubtedly picked up by the Philistines during the period of wandering from their homeland to Southern Palestine, thus indicating the roundabout way they took before they settled. Finally, the Philistines

did not settle in a vacuum. Their contacts with the local Canaanite population are clearly reflected in the fact that they adopted some pottery shapes — notably jugs, juglets, and flasks — from the Canaanite repertoire. Thus, the Philistines used an eclectic repertoire of pottery, composed of different vessels of different origins. This stands in marked contrast to the local pottery, which developed directly from the previous Late Bronze style. The decoration of the Philistine pottery is also of a hybrid nature. As with the shape, the predominant features of decoration are in the Mycenaean tradition. Most typical is a drawing of a stylized swan which sometimes turns its head backwards and peeks under its wings. Typical also are geometrical designs, such as circles, spirals, and chessboards arranged in a frieze around the body of the vessels. An unusual motif is the lotus flower painted on the necks of some jugs. This motif was undoubtedly borrowed from Egypt.

All these decorative motives do not appear on the local indigenous pottery. Not only are the motives foreign, but the whole concept of painting on pottery is alien to the local potter, who produced mostly plain vessels. The few vessels which were decorated exhibit rather crude designs, mostly groups of lines, which are a far cry from the exquisite swans and geometric designs of the

Philistine pottery. It is clear that the Philistines brought the tradition of pottery painting from their homeland. Their pottery is one of the most artistic ever produced on Palestinian soil.

In the early stages of Philistine settlement, during the 12th century BC, their typical pottery was covered with a white slip and their rich designs were painted in red and black. Later on, however, there was a marked deterioration in the quality of the Philistine pottery and a strong trend towards assimilation with the local traditions. Crude spirals painted in black on a group of deep bowls are the last echoes of the short lived Philistine episode in the history of the country.

b. *Pottery Contradicting Historical Data*

The transition between the Late Canaanite and the Early Israelite pottery is an interesting case, in which pottery changes bear upon historical problems of the first order of importance. It is a historical fact that the Israelites came out of Egypt, took over the land of Canaan, destroyed the Canaanite culture and established themselves in its stead.

Degenerated Philistine krater, note painted spirals, 11th-10th centuries BC

The commonly accepted date for the Israelite conquest is the second half of the 13th century BC. A detailed investigation of the pre-conquest pottery assemblages with post-conquest ones shows a marked and surprising similarity. If the Canaanite population was actually wiped out and replaced by an Israelite population, we would have expected to find a drastic change in the pottery styles.

But since this is not the case, explanations had to be given. It is supposed that the Israelites came to Canaan without any craft tradition. In Egypt they were slaves doing construction work, and afterwards spent many years roaming in the desert. When they started to settle in their new homeland, they quickly learned from the Canaanite survivors how to produce pottery, and naturally adopted their techniques and styles. Only many years later did the Israelites start to deviate from the Canaanite tradition and create pottery with a marked stamp of individuality.

The great impact of Canaanite pottery on that of the early Israelites was also interpreted as reflecting a large scale assimilation of the indigenous Canaanite population with the Israelite newcomers. This interpretation, based only on pottery and without any indication in the Bible, can open up new vistas in understanding the processes of conquest and settlement of the Israelites in Canaan.

c. *Pottery as the Only Data*

Probably the most drastic change in Palestinian pottery occurred in the Middle Bronze I period (2100–1900 BC). This phase in the history of Palestine follows the total destruction of the urban culture which flourished throughout the 3rd millennium. The Middle Bronze I pottery had very little in common with that of the previous, Early Bronze period. The break in tradition which has occurred between the two is the most severe in the history of the country, and probably represents an almost total replacement of the population.

The pottery of the Middle Bronze I people is characterized by its outstanding technique, its shapes, and its decorations. The vessels are made of a pale, greenish clay, so typical that it has turned into one of the criteria for identifying the ware of this period. This colour, which stands in marked contrast to the warm pink of the Early Bronze pottery, probably resulted from a special composition of clay and special conditions maintained in the firing kiln. The potter's wheel was known to the Middle Bronze I potters, but they used it only to form necks and rims of vessels which they attached to hand-made, often irregularly shaped bodies. The Early Bronze pottery is largely handmade. The prominent shape

Pottery vessels of the Middle Bronze I period, 2100–1900 BC

of the Middle Bronze I pottery as a whole is the sphere. Round jars, bowls and bottles are common, and even the large flat bases do not seem to spoil the spherical impression. The paleness of the clay is echoed in the paleness of the decoration. Slip and painting were unknown. On the other hand, Early Bronze pottery is characterized by an abundance of red slipped vessels. The most popular ornaments of the new pottery are groups of combed or incised lines, executed with the aid of either a fork-like tool with three to five teeth or a sharp wooden or metal pin, and applied mainly on the shoulders of the vessels. Handles are few and plastic decorations non-existent. The whole repertoire gives an impression of marked austerity, reflecting the poverty of the Middle Bronze I people who lived a nomadic or semi-nomadic life.

It is interesting to note that a very few

A chalice from Ur, 24th-22nd centuries BC

elements, notably the wavy handle characteristic to the Early Bronze period pottery, did survive, and appear on Middle Bronze I vessels. Do these elements prove that the previous, Early Bronze population was not wiped out completely, but that a few people survived the holocaust, joined the invaders and contributed something to their pottery? This is an attractive theory, but it is based on very little evidence.

The Middle Bronze I pottery is closely affiliated to pottery vessels commonly used in Mesopotamia and north Syria at this time. These could therefore be regarded as the homelands of newcomers, or at least as the regions which they passed during their wanderings, before they appeared on the Palestinian scene. Since we have no written historical document, this is as much as pottery can tell us about the people of this turbulent phase.

5. POTTERY AND INTERNATIONAL TRADE

An altogether different picture of pottery groups leads to reconstructing the existence of international trade relations. An archaeological picture of trade does not call for a change of the pottery repertoire, but rather for the appearance of limited numbers of foreign type vessels. If these types are found to be the common pottery of another region, then that region could be regarded as an exporter of pottery vessels, and the first region as an importer. Imported pottery does not replace the regular, indigenous pottery, but it supplements the repertoire with better, more artistic vessels. These sometimes serve as containers for some substance which was the desired commodity rather than the vessel itself.

Contrary to what one might assume from the fragility of fired clay, pottery vessels were among the most common commodities on the international market in ancient times. Large quantities of pottery vessels were transported both by land and by sea routes, testifying to lively trade relations between countries in antiquity. Very little had actually remained, however, of these commodities, either because they were immediately consumed or because they disintegrated during the long period that has passed since they went out of use and were buried in the debris of ruined settlements. Pottery, because of its absolute resistibility to all agents of destruction, is often the only evidence that remained to international commerce. The detailed study of pottery is therefore of the utmost importance in tracing the commercial activities of ancient days.

An intriguing problem connected with international trade is which vessels were traded as containers for some commodity and which were exported for their own intrinsic value. As a rule, it seems that vessels of a closed form such as jars, jugs, or juglets, especially if not decorated, served as packaging for some contents. On the other hand, more artistic vessels, particularly of an open form such as bowls or cups, were transported and traded for their own qualities.

a. *Pottery as Packaging Material*

It is generally assumed that the plain, closed vessels served as packaging for agricultural products. The large vessels, with wide mouths most probably contained solid or dry foodstuffs, while narrow mouthed jugs or bottles contained liquids. What were the agricultural products which played an important role on the international market and were shipped in clay vessels? One cannot be absolutely sure since the content of the vessels has long since disappeared and evaporated. It seems possible, however, that the main products were grain, wine and olive oil, the staple foodstuff of ancient times. Olive oil was also used as a base for medical and cosmetic products as well as fuel for lamps, and was therefore one of the most important commodities on the market. Grain, wine, and oil were commonly used in antiquity but they also

Tomb excavation in the Agora (market place) of Athens. Note Canaanite jar

had additional value as products for international trade because they do not spoil easily. They could therefore withstand the long journey by land or sea routes from the producer to the customer, and the lack of any cooling or preserving facilities on the way as well as in the markets and homes. If this assumption is true, pottery jars and jugs make it possible to trace flows of agricultural products from one country to another.

A good example of the role of pottery vessels as containers on the international market is the wide diffusion of the so-called Canaanite jars of the Late Bronze period. The shape of this medium-sized two-handled jar is an example of successful designing of useful vessels. Its thick walled body, sharp shoulders and thick bottomed base are all properly designed for easy handling, stacking, and transporting. This Canaanite jar, which was transported by sea rather than by land routes, was found in considerable numbers in many towns in Egypt as well as in towns in Greece such as Mycenae and Athens. These jars are clear evidence of the lively trade that was carried on between Canaan as an exporter and Egypt and Greece as importers of agricultural products.

A lively illustration to the exporting

activities of agricultural products of Canaanite merchants of this period is a wall painting from a tomb at Thebes in Egypt. The painting shows two ships, manned by Canaanites, tied to the docks of an Egyptian port. The merchants are shown unloading the cargo of the ships, mainly lidded and sealed Canaanite jars, while Egyptian officials seated near by weigh and record the merchandise.

While it is universally accepted that the regular, utilitarian jars and jugs contained staple foodstuffs, the contents of the small juglets, also traded frequently on the international market, are not known. They are usually described under the general term "perfumes" and "cosmetic oils". The theory presented by R. S. Merrillees (*Antiquity* Vol. XXXVI No. 144 Dec. 1962, pp. 287–92) regarding the possible content of a special kind of juglet is therefore very interesting. These juglets, known as Base Ring juglets, were produced in Cyprus in the Late Bronze period and exported in vast quantities to all countries of the Eastern Mediterranean. It is clear that these juglets were designed to contain liquids, since their tall narrow necks could permit only the flow of liquids when emptied. Merrillees found a striking resemblance between the shape of the Base Ring juglets and that of the capsule of the poppy plant, the source of

opium both in ancient times and today. He therefore suggested that the juglets were designed to contain opium dissolved in liquid, and that their shape was intended as an easily recognizable trademark for the customers of these early days, who were largely illiterate and therefore could not make use of written labels. Opium was widely used in ancient

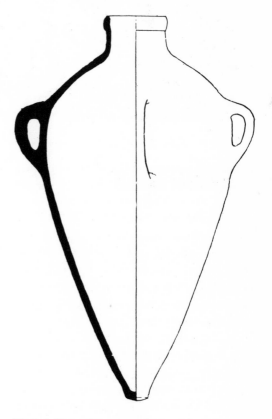

Typical Canaanite storage jar

The unloading of pottery vessels from a Canaanite ship, an Egyptian tomb painting.

times, particularly as a sedative for wounds and for crying children. This is very clear from the study of Egyptian documents, and thus the use of opium was probably as widespread as the use of aspirin today. This would explain the great popularity of the Cypriot juglets in all countries on the Eastern Mediterranean shore, where vast numbers of specimens were found in settlements and graves of the second half of the 2nd millennium BC.

b. *Pottery Vessels as Luxury Items*

Alongside pottery which served as containers for different products, many types of vessels were undoubtedly traded and cherished as luxury items for the aesthetic qualities of their shape and decoration.

During the Late Bronze period, the town of Mycenae in the Peloponnese peninsula in southern Greece specialized in manufacturing high grade pottery

Above: A drawing of a Poppy capsule

Right: Cypriot juglet in the form of a Poppy capsule

ly simple concentric lines tastefully spaced around their bodies. Particularly striking is a unique one-handled kylix of an early Mycenaean style known as Mycenaean II types, decorated with ivy leaves. While the closed vessels might have contained some luxury item such as perfumes, the open kylix was undoubtedly shipped empty.

An outstanding vessel was discovered lately in the excavations of the ancient city of Dan in northern Canaan. This is a complete "charioteer krater" of the type found in large numbers in the eastern Mediterranean countries, especially in Cyprus. Fewer kraters of this type have been found in mainland

Mycenaean kylix, 15th century BC

vessels. These excellent wheel-made and highly fired vessels won great popularity abroad, and large quantities of them were exported to all Eastern Mediterranean countries. The most popular shapes were an open, two handled drinking cup known as a kylix, a small, pear-shaped jar, a box-shaped vessel called a pyxis, a stirrup-jar which is an unusually shaped globular vessel with two necks, one false and one open, and a globular pilgrim flask. These elegant vessels were made of very fine clay and decorated with geometric designs, main-

Mycenaean charioteer krater

Cypriot "milk bowl"

Greece, although both the shape of the vase and style of decoration unmistakably reflect Mycenaean traditions. The vessel is ornamented with a double scene of two charioteers driving through imaginary scenery. This scene derives from the famous frescoes which adorned the walls of palaces of the king and noblemen of Mycenaean civilization.

The Late Bronze period export of pottery from Cyprus was not limited only to Base Ring juglets which possibly contained opium. The Base Ring pottery family also included larger jugs as well as open bowls with wish-bone shaped handles and bull-shaped vessels. All the vessels of this family were made of a dark clay which is highly fired to give a typical metallic ring. The vessels are decorated with raised or painted lines. Another internationally popular vessel is a semi-hemispherical bowl with a wish-bone shaped handle. These bowls are slipped with a white slip which gave them the name "milk bowls", and are decorated on the outside with a ladder pattern painted in brown. To this family of pottery, known as the White Slip family, belongs another jug which is much rarer than the milk bowl.

Red-Figured Attic vase, 5th century BC

All the pottery produced in Cyprus for export was handmade. This fact is surprising and hard to understand, since ordinary Cypriot pottery used in Cyprus itself was made on the wheel.

The case of the Greek vases of the Classical period is probably the best known example of export and trade in pottery vessels as luxury items. Their beautiful shapes and especially their exquisite decoration won the Greek vases an international appeal and many specimens of these vessels are found in all inhabited countries of the time.

Greek vessels made their first appearance in the Eastern Mediterranean regions already towards the end of the 7th century BC. In these early days, the vessels were all produced in Rhodes and eastern Greece. During the 6th century BC, Athenian potters learned the technique of painting black figures on pottery vessels from the potters of the town of Corinth and soon their products reached a superior quality. Athenian pottery started to dominate the international scene, and by the end of the 6th century and through the 5th and 4th centuries BC, Athens monopolized

Right: The Ishtar Gate of Babylon

Overleaf left: Rakka ware dish

Overleaf right: Greek Red-Figured vase

the world market in pottery vessels.

The Athenian export included three most popular types of ware — the Black Figured, the Red Figured, and the Black Polished. The common vessels of the decorated Figured wares were kraters, oil jugs known as *lekitoi* and cups. The Black Polished ware consisted mainly of closed oil lamps and open bowls. The superior Athenian pottery vessels were found in every settlement of the period in all Near Eastern countries, from Cyprus to south Arabia, from Mesopotamia to southern Egypt.

It seems that the Athenian vessels were imported to the east through a few port towns in Cyprus, Egypt, and the Levantine coast. The main port of entry for the Athenian products in the East was El-Mina on the north Syrian coast. Shiploads of vessels were transported in Greek ships to the port warehouses, where they were sorted according to shapes and decoration and sent by land routes to the inland regions of Syria and Mesopotamia.

c. *Trade or Migration?*

The vast quantities of imported pottery vessels from Cyprus, Mycenae, and later on from Athens found in all the countries of the eastern Mediterranean have led some archaeologists to wonder if they might not reflect migration of settlers rather than international commercial activities. It was suggested that Mycenaean immigrants established settlements on the island of Cyprus, and there they specialized in the production of Mycenaean-style pottery vessels tailored to the taste of the oriental customers on the Levantine coast. It is also possible that groups of Cypriots, including many artisans, established themselves in coast towns of Canaan and produced there the traditional and popular pottery. As for the Athenian products, it is accepted that all the ware was made in Athens itself, and the secrets of production were well guarded. Any settlement of Athenians in Near Eastern countries seem to have been inhabited by merchants rather than by artisans and potters.

Methods of analysing pottery on the basis of shape, decoration and technique cannot give absolute answers to the question of the origin of vessels, because stylistic elements can be transferred from place to place. The natural sciences, especially chemistry and geology, have also come to the aid of archaeology. Chemical techniques make it possible to identify the different particles which compose clay, even those particles that do not amount to more than a trace. It is these trace elements which serve as the "identity card" of the clay, since they are present in different amounts in

Left: Japanese tea bowl

different places. By studying the chemical composition of pottery sherds, it is possible to find out which sherds are produced from local clays and which are foreign to the area. A comparison of these foreign sherds with others from different locations would point to the place where their clay originated. This, in turn, would tell us where they were produced. This conclusion is based on the assumption that it is not the clay — the heavy and bulky raw material — which is transported, but rather the final product, namely the vessels. If, for example, the clay of Mycenaean vessels found in Cyprus proves to be of a Greek type not common to Cyprus, it would be clear that this pottery was actually produced in Greece and exported to Cyprus and not produced in Cyprus by Mycenaean settlers who kept the traditions of their homeland.

Pottery sherds excavated in the town of Ashdod on the southern coast of Palestine were found to be very similar in style and decoration to the ones found in Cyprus, and thus were supposed to have been imported from Cyprus. These pottery sherds, of the Mycenaean III Cl type, were recently examined by chemical techniques (F. Astro., I. Perlman and M. Dotan, Mycenaean III Cl ware from Tel Ashdod. *Archaeometry* 13, part 2, August 1971, pp. 169–76). Their chemical composition proved that these sherds were made of local clay, and therefore were produced locally. On the basis of the chemical composition it is now suggested that people of Cypriot origin settled in Ashdod towards the end of the 1st millennium BC and used locally found clay to produce pottery in the style and tradition of their homeland. The hypothesis of trade relations between Cyprus and Ashdod has to be ruled out.

Chemical tests of this nature, which are still only in early stages of development, promise to add a new dimension to the question of trade and settlement so important to the proper understanding of ancient civilizations.

6. POTTERY AND CHRONOLOGY

One of the ultimate aims of the archaeologist is to determine the dates in which various buildings and objects he finds were produced and used. By so doing, he can relate his finds to known historical events and possibly discover who built the city he is excavating, who destroyed it, and under whose reign the various objects found there were produced.

There are two systems for dating archaeological finds. One is the system of relative chronology, which enables the archaeologist to arrange his material in sequence by determining which artefact is older and which is newer. He can place his material in sequence without actually determining exactly when each object was produced and used. Fixing accurate dates is the task of the other system, which is known as absolute chronology. Pottery is an important element in both systems.

a. *Pottery and Relative Chronology*

The system of relative chronology is based on the way in which most archaeological material is deposited, namely in layers stratified one on top of the other, each layer representing a settlement on the ruins of the one below it. The mound which is created by the accumulation of many layers of ruined settlements is called a "tel" in the Middle East. As the excavator works on his tel, he peels off layer after layer, thus going backwards in time, since the top layer is obviously later than the one deposited under it. Careful recording of the nature of the different finds in each layer gives the archaeologist a sequence of the life of the tel, and reveals to him the changes that have occurred in the various artefacts and objects with the passing of time. Pottery is found in profusion in all strata and is therefore most valuable for such a careful study. The archaeologist will be able to establish the fact that a certain type of vessel is earlier than

another type, but later than a third. Many years of excavations and patient recording have enabled the archaeologists to establish a reliable sequence of almost every type of pottery vessel found in excavations.

Heinrich Schliemann, the first archaeologist who ventured to excavate a mound in his search for Homeric Troy, payed some attention to the existence of pottery with distinctive decorative styles, despite the fact that he had the great luck of discovering numerous precious and much more beautiful objects. The credit for recognizing the great importance of pottery for dating purposes, however, belongs to Sir W. M. Flinders Petrie. During his many years of work in many Egyptian sites, Petrie also excavated numerous graves. Since graves were usually used only once, everything that is found in them — offerings to the dead, various objects with which the dead were equipped for their afterlife — can be classified as a tomb group representing a short period of time. The trouble with excavation of graves is that they are not stratified one on top of the other, but rather found one near the other, with no obvious order. Thus Petrie was soon faced with vast quantities of pottery and other objects from graves, without any clue to their date. He knew only that they were all earlier than the unification of Egypt under one

Diagram of Egyptian pre-Dynastic pottery vessels demonstrating sequence dating system.

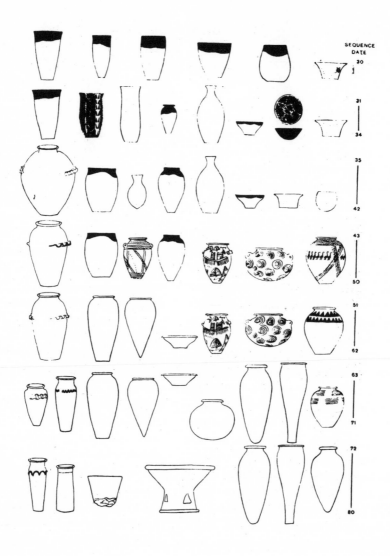

SEQUENCE
DATE

20

31

34

35

42

43

50

51

62

63

71

72

80

Profiles of characteristic types of pottery vessels from the principal archaeological periods in Palestine.

1. Chalcolithic period　　3. Middle Bronze Age　　5. Iron Age I　　7. Iron Age III　　9. Roman period
2. Early Bronze Age　　　4. Late Bronze Age　　　6. Iron Age II　　8. Hellenistic period　　10. Byzantine period

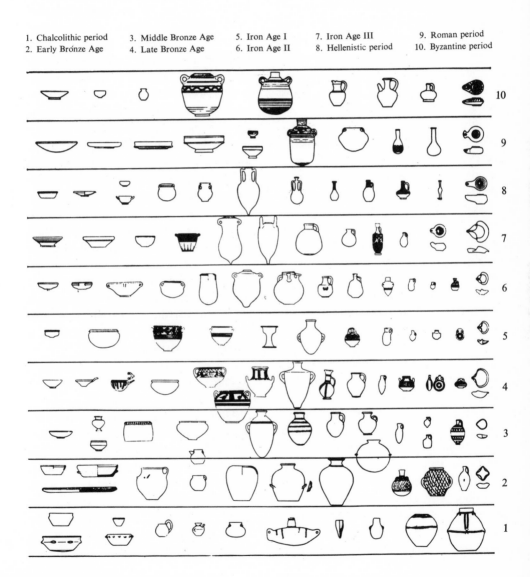

king, from a period known as the pre-Dynastic period.

Petrie decided to sort out the pottery vessels by stylistic criteria, and divided these vessels into nine groups according to their shape or special decoration. Petrie noticed that one attribute, a wavy handle on the body of the jars, shows variation and change. He put these handles first in a chronological sequence, with the functional handles first and the degenerated ones last. With the wavy handles as a criterion, Petrie arranged the pottery of the tomb groups in fifty classes which he arbitrarily numbered from 30 to 80, leaving room for additional earlier or later groups which might be discovered. Thus a class of pottery numbered 40 will be earlier than one numbered 50. This system is known as Sequence Dating and is the first chronological tool based on pottery. It should be noted, however, that sequence dating does not give an absolute date, nor does it establish the length of time of each individual class.

Petrie saw such a powerful criterion in pottery that, when excavating Tell el-Hesi, a mound on the southern coastal plain of Palestine, he prophesied that "once settle the pottery of a country and the key is in our hands for all future explorations. A single glance at a mound of ruins will show as much to anyone who knows the styles of the pottery as

weeks of work may reveal to the beginner" (*Tell el-Hesi*, p. 40). Professor Myers went as far as suggesting that "even from horseback an observant traveller can often assign approximate limits of date to an ancient site in the country" (*ibid*, p. 114). In his excavations at Tell el-Hesi, Petrie has established the relation between the various strata of the mound and the different types of pottery he found. He built the sequence dating of Palestinian pottery, which many years of excavations in Palestine since his days have refined and elaborated.

The story of the storage jar, always an essential household vessel, will illustrate the changes that occur even in the most elementary shape and demonstrate how an archaeologist, by developing a sharp eye for minute details, can trace these changes and utilize them as a criterion for dating.

b. *Pottery and Absolute Chronology*

Although pottery played a major role in establishing relative chronology, absolute dating is a direct function of written documents. Pottery vessels can serve as indicators of absolute dates either when they bear the name of a known and dated personality, or when they are found in relation to other objects which are clearly dated. In this way of historical dating, pottery has no value of its own. But owing to its indestructability and wide diffusion, it enables the archaeologist to establish contact between one place or group which is dated and another which is not. The absolute chronology of Egypt is well established because of the numerous documents giving names of kings, duration of their reign, and events which occurred during their period of reign found there. In the archaeological study of countries of the Ancient Near East, it is very useful to discover connections which have existed with Egypt, connections which can be traced by finding Egyptian objects outside of Egypt or foreign objects on Egyptian soil. From the 1st millennium BC onward, the absolute dates of Assyria, Babylonia, Greece and Rome among others take the place of Egypt as sources of accurate dating. A few examples will illustrate the place of pottery and its importance for absolute dating.

The earliest definite contact between Canaan and Egypt dates to the very beginning of recorded history. In Tel 'Erany, a prominent mound in the central plain of Palestine, a fortified town existed during the early phases of the Early Bronze period. In layer V of the tel, pottery of clear Egyptian origin suddenly appears, consisting mostly of pear-shaped pots coated with a fine, white, highly burnished slip and tall, cylindrical jars, some with a degenerated wavy handle, so important in establishing the sequence dating system.

One sherd from a shoulder of a pot has graffito of hieroglyphic signs incised on it This graffito has been deciphered as the name of King Narmer, who was the first king to unite upper and lower Egypt and the founder of the first Egyptian dynasty of kings. Since we know the dates of King Narmer (*ca.* 3100 BC), we thus have a data for strata V of Tel 'Erany and subsequently for all similar material found elsewhere.

Contacts with Egypt existed throughout the period of the first Egyptian dynasty of kings. Pottery vessels, mainly jugs and jars of clear Canaanite style and workmanship, were found in tombs of kings, noblemen and simple people dating from the first Egyptian dynasty of kings. It is thus clear that this group of vessels, known as the Abydos Ware, after the site of Abydos in Egypt, was exported from Canaan to Egypt at a very early date, between 2900 and 2700 BC. The most common vessel of this group is a jug, usually red slipped and burnished but sometimes painted with dark brown paint on a background of white slip. A peculiar feature of some of these jugs is a high stump base. The jugs are well made, and are fired to such a high temperature that they give a metallic sound when knocked upon. Another

Pottery sherd incised with the hieroglyphic signs of King Narmer

Abydos ware

vessel of exported Abydos Ware is a large jar painted with triangles, dots, and semi-circles in red on the natural colour of the body. In Canaan, this type of jar was discovered only in the town of Arad, which was one of the flourishing urban centres of the period. Another type of jar is a highly fired, thin-walled vessel decorated with an attractive combed pattern. The jars, which contained some kind of solid food, maybe grain, and the jugs, which held some liquid such as olive oil or wine, testify to a lively trade between Canaan and Egypt in the early part of the 3rd millennium BC. The Abydos Ware, so clearly dated, is the key to the absolute dates of the Early Bronze Age in Canaan, and particularly of the second phase of this age in which the ware was produced and exported.

A third instance in which pottery is crucial for setting absolute dates occurred within the Late Bronze Age. In 1379 BC, an Egyptian king named Amenophis IV rose to the throne. Six years later, after initiating a religious revolution in the country by elevating the sun god Aten to the position of the one and only god of Egypt, the king, under the new name Akhenaton which reflects his new religious beliefs, moved his capital to a totally new city, now known as El Amarna. Less than two decades later, in 1362 BC, the king died and his capital was deserted. Everything found in the ruins of El Amarna will therefore date from a well defined period of short duration. The population of El Amarna used a variety of pottery vessels, including pottery imported from the town of Mycenae in Greece. This type of pottery, classified as the Mycenaean III/A type, is found in many sites in Canaan, Syria, Cyprus, and of course in Greece, its homeland. Wherever it is found, it is thus accurately dated to the El Amarna period, and in turn dates all the other pottery and objects found together with it. Through this type of Mycenaean pottery, it is possible to correlate finds over wide areas, including Greece itself, which does not have any other means of obtaining absolute dates for such an early period. Mycenaean III/A pottery, dated accurately in El Amarna, has thus become one of the most important pivots on which Near Eastern chronology of the 2nd millennium BC is based.

During the second half of the 1st millennium BC, large numbers of pottery jars were shipped from various towns around the Aegean Sea to most inhabited countries of that time. These jars, which probably contained wine, had an elongated body ending in a point, a tall neck and two handles. Since quantities of liquids were expressed in ancient times in terms of clay jars — for example, when the Sinopean population presented

Xenophon and his army with 1500 jars of wine — it was essential to supervise the correct capacity of the jars. The capacity was therefore endorsed by stamped impressions on the handles of these wine jars. Usually both handles were stamped. The stamp on one handle was the name of an eponym — the priest in whose term of office it was produced. The name of the eponym, preceded by the Greek preposition "epi" meaning "in the term of", thus served as a date. The stamp on the other handle was the name of the manufacturer of the vessels, or more probably the name of the commissioner responsible for the output of standard products, and was thus the proper endorsement.

Over 100,000 stamped handles have been found in almost all the countries of the Mediterranean and the Near East. Through a careful study of the change in the shape of the jars as well as the names of both eponyms and commissioners, a sequence of handles was built. The largest series of handles, that of Rhodian jars, was produced and exported during the term of office of 177 eponyms, who served between the latter part of the 4th century and the year 44 BC.

The starting point for the study of the sequence of Rhodian stamped handles was a deposit of handles found in the foundation of a building in the city of Pergamon, dated to 220–180 BC. The handles included names of about 40 eponyms. Further excavations in towns with clear dates of foundation or destruction supplemented further information. Thus, handles found in Alexandria cannot antedate 331 BC, when the city was founded, and handles from Carthage cannot postdate the city's destruction by the Romans in 146 BC. Thus an eponym's name found in Carthage but not in Pergamon would date between 180 and 146 BC.

Another way of identifying and dating eponyms is by correlating them with eponyms mentioned in other sources, especially stone inscriptions. The sequence can be further controlled by the names stamped on handles of the intact jars. An eponym and commissioner mentioned on one jar are obviously contemporary. The name of the same commissioner appearing with that of another eponym would indicate that the two eponyms cannot be far removed in time.

Much confusion arose from the fact that more than one eponym was named by the same name. The readiest criterion for distinguishing between men of the same name but different generations is the change that occurred in the shape of the jars and especially in the shape of the handles themselves. It is possible to trace the change from rounded or arched handles to handles with a sharp angle.

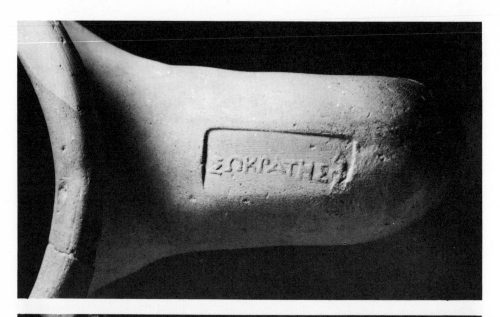

Handles of Rhodian wine jars

Angular handles were not in vogue before the later part of the 3rd century BC. Through the 2nd and 1st centuries BC, the angle tends to sharpen, while the workmanship of the jar gradually deteriorates. The sequential list of eponyms is now more or less complete and any new handle found can be checked against this list and can be accurately dated.

c. *Modern Physics and Pottery Dating*

After World War II, advanced methods of scientific research began to be applied to the study of ancient civilizations, and especially to the problems of dating ancient materials. These methods are based not on historical information, but on the nature of the materials themselves, on the changes which they undergo with time, and on the information which is stored in them.

The best known scientific method for dating archaeological finds is the Carbon 14 method. This method examines the amount of the radioactive element C14 which is found in the sample tested. It then calculates the amount that has disintegrated and thus establishes the length of time that has passed since the sample died. The Carbon 14 test, however, can be applied only to organic matter, wood, bones, straw mats, and cotton or flax textiles, since only organic matter

absorbs carbon and changes it into the radioactive C14 when it is alive. Since pottery is made of inorganic materials, this method is of no use for establishing its dates. The vast quantities of ancient pottery were thus worthless for scientific tests until recently, when completely new methods were developed.

One of the most promising new methods is thermoluminescence dating. This method was first presented in 1968, and has since been refined and elaborated. It is based on the fact that every material is exposed to radiation both from cosmic rays and from radio-active sources on the earth. The amount of radiation the material absorbs depends on the length of time the material was exposed. When the material is heated, it emits the radiation which was trapped in it. This emitted energy can be measured and thus it is possible to determine the length of time the material was exposed to radiation. If the material contains phosphors, the absorbed radiation will be emitted in the form of light rays.

During the process of firing the pottery the clay, which contains certain amounts of phosphors, is heated to such high temperatures that all the radiation it absorbed up to the time of firing escapes. Upon cooling, the clay starts a new cycle of absorbing radiation. The light rays which it emits in the laboratories will measure the length of time which has passed since the vessel was fired, and thus give the date of its production. The procedures of choosing the elements for such a test, and the means by which to measure the emission of light rays, are complicated. Scientists are able to date pottery with a 15 per cent margin of error, which is quite considerable. Future refining of the method will probably reduce this margin. This method is especially important where no historical documents are available, such as the pre-Roman Empire period or pre-Colombian America.

The thermoluminescence dating system is applied not only to ascertain the correct dating of groups, but also to establish the authenticity of disputed items, a procedure much needed in museums. A small emission of light rays would indicate that a piece of pottery is new, and therefore not authentic. These tests have enabled the Ashmolean Museum, for example, to discover forgeries of vessels which were thought to have come from Neolithic sites in Anatolia.

Deer-shaped vase, Amlash ware, Iran, 10th-8th centuries BC

ILLUSTRATION SOURCES

The Israel Department of Antiquities and Museums, P. 11; 25; 29; 33–35; 59–61; 73–76; 84; 85; 88; 91. Museum of Fine Arts, Boston, H. L. Pierce Fund, P. 14. Photo W. Braun, Jerusalem, P. 15. Museum für Kunst und Gewerbe, Hamburg, P. 16. Photo D. Harris, Jerusalem, P. 17, Field School, Kfar Etzion, P. 18; 26. Kodansha International Ltd., P. 20; 21; 27. G. Edelstein, Jerusalem, P. 22. Museum of the American Indian, Heye Foundation N.Y., P. 22. British Museum, London, P. 24; 64; 66. The Metropolitan Museum of Art, Rogers Fund, P. 24; 42. R. Kimchi, Jerusalem, P. 31; 37; 38. American School of Archaeology, Athens, P. 39. The Museum, Devizes, P. 40. American Museum of Natural History, N. Y., P. 41. Hirmer Fotoarchiv, Munich, P. 36; 44. Cambridge University, Cambridge, P. 46. Prof. Yigael Yadin, Jerusalem, P. 52–55; 57. The Oriental Institute, University of Chicago, P. 57. Agora Excavation Athens, P. 70. Archaeological Receipts Funds, Ministry of Science, Greece, P. 67 Smithsonian Institution, Freer Gallery of Art, Washington D.C., P. 68. Ruth Amiran, Jerusalem, P. 81. Vorderasiatisches Museum, Berlin, P. 65.

INDEX